Published by LIFE Publishing
P.O. Box 982000 Fort Worth, Texas 76182.

ISBN 13: 978-0-9819567-0-1
Printed in the United States of America.
First Printing: May 2009.

Racing Jesus

to the hurting

JAMES ROBISON

Table of Contents

"I want to spend the rest of my life racing Jesus to the hurting, the suffering and the fallen."

Racing Jesus to the Side of the Hurting

Dreams can be powerful things. Not the kind you have when you are asleep, though they can be very powerful – just ask the prophet Daniel or the wise men of the Christmas story. But the kind of dreams I am talking about keep you up at night, the kind you can't get off your mind.

These dreams keep you going through tough times. They seem unattainable, but in your heart you know they'll make the world a better place.

I have had a few dreams of my own over the years. Some were big world-changing dreams like helping provide clean drinking water by drilling fresh water wells, or to feed and minister to one million starving children. Every week, by God's grace, we're well on our way to reaching both goals.

But it was something Pastor Erwin McManus asked me on our *LIFE TODAY* television program that really grabbed my attention. I love Erwin's passion for people; he is a provocative thinker, and what he says often challenges me and gets me thinking. He asked this simple question, "If your dreams were fulfilled, what difference would it make?" In other words, if your dreams come true, whose life does it make better?

When I first heard this question, I was 65 years old and my beautiful wife Betty and I had been married for 46 years. We have seen God do some pretty amazing and miraculous things over the course of our life together, but we're still dreaming and we're still asking God to change us and work through us. While we may have been used by God, He still has so much for us to do . . . and that's why we still dream.

He asked this simple question, "If your dreams were **fulfilled,** what difference would it make?" In other words, if your **dreams come true,** whose life does it make better?

"We **still dream** over the entire course of our lives."

For many years now, I have prayed for the family of God to begin to truly love each other just as Jesus prayed we would. Jesus prayed for Christians around the world to be perfected in unity with God and one another. His dream is for the church to be healthy and vibrant and, consequently, to have an undeniable impact on the whole world for Christ.

John 17:20-21 says, *"My prayer is not for them alone. I pray also for those who will believe in me through their message, that all of them may be one, Father, just as you are in me and I am in you. May* they also be in us so that the world may believe that you have sent me."

In Luke 4, Jesus started His earthly ministry at the synagogue in Nazareth by reading saiah 61:1-2 – . . . *He has sent me to b'nd up the brokenhearted, to prociaim freedom for the captives and release from darkness for the prisoners.* Jesus came to serve those who are hurting, captive or trapped in darkness. His endless and unconditional love is what motivates Him. He's always running to people's side, filled with compassion and ready to help in a time of need.

My dream is to see God's people racing Jesus to the side of the hurting and to the aid of the suffering.

Now, "racing Jesus" might be a strange image without some form of explanation, so let me tell you what I mean. We pass hurting and wounded people every day. We pass them in the grocery store, at the bank, in our offices in schools and in the halls of our church. So what do we do?

Our human inclination is to run *from* them, but Jesus, you see, He always runs *to* them. You and can never outrun our Lord anywhere, no matter how hard we try, but if Jesus is going to be the first one there, we should be right on His heels. Racing Jesus to hurting people, particularly those of the family of God, would help unite us and make us one, just as our Savior prayed we would be.

As I said earlier, racing Jesus is not something that comes naturally. As human beings, we tend to want to run from people with problems rather than to them. The funny thing is, when we're honest, we realize all of us have problems, all of us have times when we hurt deeply.

As with every race, there is a right way to race Jesus and a wrong way. It is my heart's desire and prayer that Christians everywhere will be empowered by the Holy Spirit to learn the right way to race Jesus to the side of the broken and hurting.

Technique Can Outrun Talent

Technique Can Outrun Talent

People who run in the Olympics and world championships are first-class athletes. They are able to perform at the level they do because of God-given talent, years of agonizing training, and a finely-tuned technique. Often, those who have never competed at such a high level do not realize how much these blazing-fast human beings have trained. They've put hours and hours into learning and relearning techniques, such as how to hold their hands when running, not turning their heads, and coming out of the starting blocks faster than the competition.

Winning a race is not just about being the most talented or fastest; it's usually the runner with the best technique that crosses the finish line first.

It is much the same way when we are racing Jesus. It may not necessarily be *what* we do or say that has a positive or negative impact on people; often it is as much a matter of *how* we do things

My dream is to see God's people **racing** Jesus to the side of the hurting and to the aid of the suffering."

or say things that makes all the difference in the world. There are a lot of Christians who have many bright, intelligent and thoughtful things to say, but if they are said antagonistically and with a mean spirit, instead of enlightening and encouraging, these words only serve to polarize and offend people.

This is a lesson I have had to learn time and time again over my many years of ministry. I have said the right thing the wrong way enough times in my life, I can now look back on it and recognize my mistakes. I may have been right, but I was

This is a **lesson** I have had to **learn** time and time again over my **many years** of **ministry.** I have said the right thing the wrong way enough times, I can **now look back and recognize my mistakes.**

speaking in a way that was less than the best way to really make a difference.

Now, just because you do something the right way does not mean that it will be well received. Even if you do something the right way, you just might get crucified, and often by people you thought would be supportive. People are sinners, and as such, they have a tendency to react negatively to the truth.

When we are attempting to help those who are hurting and wounded, we must do it with compassion and a connection to the person. We must combine the truth with compassion for people. We can be very sincere, but without the truth we will just be sincerely wrong. We must be sincere in our desire to help, but we must do it in a way that is meaningful, principled and solid. Only the truth of the Gospel can ultimately bring healing and an abundant life.

We must combine the **truth** with **compassion for people.** We can be very **sincere,** but without the **truth** we will just be **sincerely wrong.**

For those in the family of God, this area is one of the greatest spiritual breakdowns of Christianity in our day and time, and really throughout history. Our failure to love one another as we should has resulted in Christian brothers and sisters viewing one another as opponents, rather than teammates working toward the same goal. Too often we have been in separate fortresses, continually firing verbal mortars at one another rather than accurately looking at ourselves as misunderstood and separated brethren. Healing urgently needs to come to the church in this area.

There are many great and wonderful conversations that should take place within the body of Christ, but we fail to race Jesus to the side of people in our spiritual family that are hurting, and so those conversations never happen. I continually pray for this healing to come.

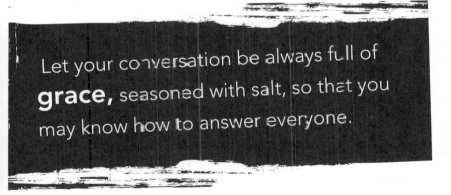

Let your conversation be always full of **grace,** seasoned with salt, so that you may know how to answer everyone.

"

All of our words are
enhanced by our relationship
with Christ."

I believe we can follow the Scriptural teaching to reason together as the body of Christ. Too often we do not sit down to reason together because we only want to prove one another wrong. In Colossians 4:6 Paul challenges us to speak with compassion as all of our words are flavored by our relationship with Christ. *Let your conversation be always full of grace, seasoned with salt, so that you may know how to answer everyone.* The family of God ought to be the one place where our words and actions are delivered in the right way. Congress, the media, Hollywood and everyday Americans ought to be able to observe how the church interacts with one another and learn from it. Regrettably, more often than not, this has not been the case.

Fortunately for us, God specializes in handing out new beginnings. It is vital to the mission of the church that we seek out and find those who are hurting and run to them. The world today has numerous problems that Jesus has already run to. Our fellow believers are hurting from loneliness, depression, anxiety and so much more. People want a new beginning, so let's race Jesus to their side – together. Remember when reaching out to those who hurt, they must be convinced you love them where they are and that you truly care about them as a person. They must not think you are simply trying to make them like you or win them to your group. Jesus demonstrated this approach when He met the woman at the well.

"Everyone who drinks this water will be thirsty again, but **whoever drinks** the water I give him will never thirst. Indeed, the water I give him will become in him a spring of water welling up to eternal life." John 4:13-14

Put Down Your Stones Before You Run

Put Down Your Stones Before You Run

Runners' outfits have gotten progressively smaller, more aerodynamic and more scientifically engineered over the years. This has all been done to reduce the weight and drag on their bodies, enabling them to run faster and faster. Other racers, such as those that race cars or horses, know all too well that any extra weight can spell doom in a timed contest. The Pharisees of Jesus' day often raced Him to hurting people, but they did it with heavy stones in their hands. If you want to race Jesus, then you first have to put down any weight that might hinder you on your journey. You must lay down your stones.

Today, just as in biblical times, there are always those ready to throw the first stone. Whether you are someone running to a hurting person or someone who is hurting and in need of help, there are those ready to judge and punish you. I know personally that when notable religious leaders have fallen over the years, brothers and sisters in

Christ raced to their side without stones in their hands. But when they got there, the fallen leader didn't want their help.

If you want to race Jesus, then you first have to put down any weight that might hinder you on your journey. You must lay down your stones.

I know, because at times I've been the one who ran only to be denied. I did not go unkindly; I went lovingly, and the people still did not respond to my attempts to offer hope and restoration. There are reasons people do not respond when we race Jesus to meet their needs. Often when a person has reached a place of recognition, respect and responsibility, they are afraid to go to others when they need help.

Where does a person like that go in order to admit they are dealing with something that would be disappointing and shocking to so many people in and out of the church? Most people, whether they're well-known or not, are afraid to be honest about their problems.

Lay down your stones.

They're afraid that if they open up, they'll either be tarred and feathered or rejected by those who hear their story and learn of their failure.

Most people, whether they're well-known or not, are afraid to be honest about their problems.

Too often when someone falls into a sin, particularly a controversial one, the rest of the family of God runs away and then leaves them hung out to dry. They end up acting more like the crowd than Jesus in the story of the woman caught in adultery from John 8.

John 8:7-9 says, When they kept on questioning him, he straightened up and said to them. "If any one of you is without sin, let him be the first to throw a stone at her." Again he stooped down and wrote on the ground. At this, those who heard began to go away one at a time, the older ones first, until only Jesus was left, with the woman still standing there.

When we are truly committed to racing Jesus to the hurting, it's not about us; it's about the ones we're running to. I am so passionate about finding ways to help people because I do not believe that I have ever met anyone who does not need help in some way. I have observed enough hurting and defeated people, and lived long enough myself, to know something about this. We are surrounded by hurting people. If we really think about this honestly, we will remember times when we have been hurting. We have all been hurt and in pain, and even if we are not right now, we will be soon. Why race Jesus? Because one day very soon, we may be hurting again too.

Some of you reading these words are dealing with a serious issue, or maybe several serious issues – compulsive spending, obsessive eating or perhaps even damaged relationships. If that is you, you probably feel defeated because you can't find a way to overcome your struggle. Because you can't control your problem, it feels even bigger than it is; it makes you feel like a hypocrite or a failure. You claim to follow a Savior who said He will set you free from bondage, yet if you are totally honest, you are still bound by these struggles. Like a prisoner you are in chains, though you'd do anything to be set free.

If this is you, you don't have to be ashamed because of your chains any longer. Someone who has the courage to stand up and say, "I have a problem," does not need to be suddenly put in their place for admitting they have an issue. The Bible never tells us to act this way toward those who are stuck in sin and despair and genuinely want help, yet too many times this is exactly what happens.

I want to be for **somebody** what I would want someone to be for me when I am **hurting.**

"Some of you reading these words are dealing with a serious issue, or maybe several serious issues – **compulsive spending,** obsessive eating or perhaps even damaged relationships. "

The Word of God tells us to confess our sins to one another so that we may be healed (see James 5:16). Confession is for the purpose of healing, not for punishment. Who would want to confess their sins in order to be stoned? Not me!

Confession is meant to remove the shame, humiliation and fear that are caused by sin, but our pride makes it difficult for us to admit our faults. Many times when people are confronted, they begin to cover up the problem, they deny the issue, they attempt to defend themselves, or even worse they attempt to deceive in order to cover up their predicament. It is all an attempt to avoid the consequences. The difficulty is that when they finally hit rock bottom and are willing to deal with their crisis, they ask themselves, "Who can I admit this to who will not organize a group of stone throwers?"

The religious people of Jesus' day were the first ones to race to the fallen, because they had a stone to throw. Its still this way today – wherever people have fallen you'll find people, far too often the religious crowd, moving in with stones in their hands. Racing Jesus means being someone others can trust, someone who has run to their side with open hands and a heart of restoration, not someone who is carrying stones.

I will **lie down and sleep** in **peace,** for **you alone,** O LORD, make me dwell in **safety.** Psalm 4:8

Be a Safe Place

During the 1992 Olympics in Barcelona, Spain, one of the strangest and most touching things happened during a hotly-contested race. Sprinter Derek Redmond of Great Britain was considered a favorite to win a medal in the 400 meter run. Halfway through the race, Redmond stopped running and reached for his leg; a torn hamstring had ended his Olympic dream almost before it had begun.

As the other racers finished, Redmond fell to his knees in agony. After a few seconds, however, he rose and attempted to finish his race by limping around the track. Suddenly, a man in the stands jumped the railing, pushed aside security and rushed to Redmond's side to give him a shoulder to lean on for the final stretch. The man, who refused to leave Redmond's side until he crossed the finish line, was his father. In this, the most crushing moment of his life as an athlete, Redmond found the safest place to be was in his father's arms.

The goal in racing Jesus is the same as that of Derek Redmond's father – give people who are hurting a safe place, a shoulder to lean on.

Christians are the body of Christ, the revelation of God on the earth, and as such our destiny is to be the strong shoulder upon which others can lean. Remember even King David struggled to find a safe place among his friends, but the Lord was his safe place. Some of us have never even learned how to be a safe place, and God may be saying that it is time to learn. I want God to use me to be part of the process of healing for people who are hurting. The last thing someone who is suffering needs is for someone to come and add to their pain.

The hurting don't want someone to come in and cast blame – they don't want someone to come in and try to fix everything right away.

Many times, being a safe place is about being there with them to listen and to understand what they're going through.

a safe place

When Jesus ran to the side of the hurting, He took the time to understand what they were going through. He wept with Mary and Martha before He raised Lazarus from the dead.

Are you the one? Are you the safe place? I have prayed this for our ministry staff at LIFE Outreach International — that anybody with a broken heart could find a safe place. This is part of the dream of health and wholeness in the family where we can truly lean on each other not on our own understanding.

As believers, being a safe place for those who are hurting does not mean we ignore sin. Most of the time the healing process will involve wrong attitudes and sinful behavior – but for someone who is hurting to let you in to this place, you have to demonstrate and even prove you can be trusted. I urge you to be that person – the kind of person God wants all of us to be – a safe place.

Run to Help, Not to Expose

Run to Help, Not to Expose

Recent disasters have introduced us to a new kind of race, the race of the first responder. First responders do not run to beat the competition; they run to save lives. Tragedies such as the terrorist attacks of 9/11, Hurricane Katrina and many others have brought the amazing lives of these heroic people to the forefront of our thoughts many times in recent years. These are the people who run into dangerous situations when everyone else is fleeing. They run carrying assistance, not video cameras. Their job is to rescue people at risk, not to describe the danger for those sitting on their couches watching television.

First responders run to help, not to expose.

A God who would sacrifice His only Son to cover your sins would not make exposing sin His top priority. He is not interested in covering up sin . . . He wants it to end. What is the point of exposing sin to those who aren't affected by it? People always want to know who is committing what sin, but it's not really their business, is it? I think the desire to expose other people's sin is why God had such a harsh word for Noah's son and for the religious leaders with the woman caught in adultery. For some reason, most people are excited to expose the sins of others, even their brothers and sisters in Christ.

> A God who would **sacrifice His only Son** to **cover your sins** would not make exposing sin His top **priority**, but for some reason, most people are **excited** to **expose** the sins of others, even their brothers and sisters in **Christ**.

Remember God's reaction to Adam and Eve in the Garden of Eden? He covered them and put clothes on them. Let me be clear here – I am not talking about hiding sin by covering it up; I am talking about dealing with the sin. There is a very clear distinction in the Bible between covering a sin and covering it up. The blood of Jesus Christ covers our sins, and the Apostle Peter, in his first epistle, says that *love covers over a multitude of sins* (1 Peter 4:8). *Covering up* a sin is not dealing with it; it is sweeping it under the rug to avoid the consequences that come along with that sin. Covering a sin is dealing with that sin in an appropriate and scriptural manner. Covering sin always involves repentance, honesty and restoration. But *covering up* a sin frequently entails dishonesty.

Now, if we won't repent, if someone approaches us to aid and not to expose and we reject that, then God may very well expose us in our pride. The Bible makes it clear in James 4:6 that *God opposes the proud but gives grace to the humble.* I don't want God to oppose me – I want Him to continue giving His grace in my life. We should always be quick to repent of our pride and encourage others to do the same. Otherwise, for our own good, God will expose our sins.

Over the years LIFE Outreach International has had many opportunities to work with, and even be, first responders during some of the different crises that have affected so many millions of people. The Lord has given us opportunities to minister in the wake of the September 11, 2001, terrorist attacks, in areas affected by hurricanes

First responders run to **help.**

Katrina and Rita, in areas affected by the powerful tsunami of 2004, and in areas of Africa where numerous atrocities and human suffering are rampant.

> Covering sin always involves repentance, honesty and restoration. But *covering up* a sin frequently entails dishonesty.

At the times of those horrific calamities, there were many people who were frantically searching for help. What they needed in first responders was aid. Some of them needed medical attention, some financial assistance, some food or water, and some just needed an ear to lster to them, but they all needed help. They needed someone to come to their aic, and to come as quickly as possible.

In larger cities with traffic problems the traffic reporters talk about something called "rubber-necking" or "onlooker slowdown." This happens whenever one side of traffic backs up, not because there is an accident, but because there is an accident on the other side of the freeway.

He gives us opportunities
to minister.

Drivers slow down and look, not because they want to help, but because they're curious; they want to see what all the flashing emergency lights are pointing to.

God opposes the proud but gives grace to the humble.

The real issue is our motivation. Are we stopping because we're curious to see how bad the "accident" in a person's life is or because we want to be seen as someone who's helping others? Or are we so focused on helping those who are hurting that we don't have time for onlooker slowdown?

Our motivation n racing Jesus should be to get to hurting people to offer compassion and love – not to expose their sin, but to assist them in dealing with it.

Don't Get Distracted in the Race

Any bird dog owner will tell you that there is nothing more focused than a good bird dog. A good bird dog knows exactly which prey it is hunting, but a poorly-trained dog wants to chase every rabbit, every squirrel, every little field lark that flies up.

If a good bird dog is hunting quail, no matter what flies up in its face, it does not stop looking for quail. A rabbit can run right across its path, and it doesn't even see the rabbit if it is looking for quail. When we are racing Jesus, we have to be the same way. We cannot afford to let things distract us from running to the side of people that are in need.

If a dog can be trained, then as loving and caring members of God's family, with God's help, we can learn to go straight ahead without paying attention to distractions.

focused.

Many Christian men and women have been distracted by their own sins and unable to help the hurting around them. Instead of racing Jesus to help others, they need someone to run to them.

Our world is saturated with negative impressions. They're on television, the radio, billboards – everywhere you look, sinful actions and desires are advertised and made to look appealing. This is why you must stay focused and remember your training. For the bird dog, rabbits, deer and the wrong kind of birds are everywhere, yet it stays true to its purpose.

You may be someone who struggles because you always compare yourself with other people you consider to be smarter, better looking or have a better personality. You are constantly measuring yourself against these other people, and you always come up short in your estimation. Maybe because of your comparisons, your problem is not that you struggle with eating too much; maybe it has caused you to have an eating disorder. God can help us learn to train every appetite. Whether it is a desire to consume too much or a compulsion to not consume enough, He is all-powerful, and our desires are subject to Him even if we feel that they are controlling our lives.

Bird dogs do not start out being able to ignore distractions. All dogs are naturally wired to see and smell anything and everything that is moving. Yet when it is trained, that same bird dog can ignore dozens of different kinds of birds and point to one single, solitary type of

Bird dogs do not start out being able to ignore distractions. All dogs are **naturally wired** to see and smell **anything** and everything that is moving. Yet when it is **trained,** that same **bird dog** can **ignore dozens of** different kinds of **birds** and **point** to one single, **solitary type of bird.**

bird. We must come before God and ask Him to help us train every appetite and desire, and after we have asked God for help, we really must ask for help from one another. Together we can help each other stay focused on Jesus, to press on toward the mark of the prize of the high calling in Christ Jesus. No matter the distraction – whether it is food, pleasure, entertainment, sports, hobbies – it does not matter. God wants us to enjoy these things, not to be controlled by them.

Highly trained bird dogs notice the rabbit or the wrong kind of bird, but they recognize it is a distraction, ignore it and keep running.

I would have given anything in the world to have heard this when I was a child, because it is so easy to be shaped by sin. The enemy will feed you thoughts and tell you to fantasize and imagine sinful acts. He will get you hooked on the wrong things, and then he will lead you wherever he wants you to go. Do not lie to yourself and pretend that there are no sinful distractions that tempt you. They are there all around us. Admit it and believe that it is not God's best for you, as you trust Him to help you keep going where He's called you.

Submit yourselves, then, to God. Resist the devil, and He Will **Flee** From You! James 4:7

He calls us from our distractions.

Follow the Right Pattern

Follow the Right Pattern

Runners who are smart learn to be the best partially by watching others who are already excellent in that endeavor. The same holds true for bankers, pastors, doctors and almost any other profession. You learn best and grow the most by patterning yourself after those who have already proven themselves successful in what you are trying to do. Racing Jesus really only requires one other runner – Jesus Himself.

The older I get, the more I realize I need to grow. There are always more and more areas where I see a need for fine tuning in my life.

When racing, Jesus you will actually be following Him.

Now, hopefully the Carpenter will just need to do some sanding here and there, and not sand blasting. I have had times in my life when God had to pull out the heavy machinery, and though I do not really like the jack hammer in my life, sometimes it is very effective.

"Pattern yourself after those who have **already** proven themselves successful."

financia

(sək ses'

result; ou

) someth

All of these things happen so that God can continue to make me after His pattern of Jesus Christ. Do you know how great He really is? He's such a wonderful, wonderful friend and Savior. Sometimes when I talk about Him, I tear up, because I know Him. I have known Him a long time, and I know Him intimately. He is so different from the people who many times claim to represent Him. He's so absolutely, magnetically attractive. I wish everyone could only see Him without the screen of worldly and religious influence and traditions of men that diffuse the truth and diminish its effect.

The Lord promised that if He was lifted up He would *"draw all men"* unto Himself (John 12:32). There is a constant need to lift up Jesus as our supreme example. We should continually realize this is a need when we see leaders who are flawed. It must be Christ who is lifted up, not men or women who can and will disappoint

When we read the Bible, which we know is the Word of God, we see that the leaders in it were flawed. So why is it that we seem so shocked when we discover that someone in our world today is incredibly flawed? The Word says it, and it is true: *We all, like sheep, have gone astray* (Isaiah 53:6). That includes me, it includes every pastor, and it includes you. It is only by the grace of God that we live, and this is why we must follow the example of the ultimate pattern of our Lord.

The Scriptures also tell us that *"There is none righteous, no, not one"* (Romans 3:10 NKJV), and by the way, that includes believers. There is only one who is good, just and righteous, and that is God. So the only goodness is godliness, and

Do you know how great He really is? He's such a wonderful, wonderful friend and Savior. He is so different from the people who many times claim to represent Him. He's so absolutely, magnetically attractive. I wish everyone could only see Him without the screen of worldly and religious influence and traditions of men that diffuse the truth and diminish its effect.

the only righteousness is *Christ in [us]*, which is *the hope of glory* (Colossians 1:27). *God forbid that [we] should boast except in the cross of our Lord Jesus*

Christ . . . (Galatians 6:14 NKJV). Jesus died to redeem us, to set us free.

We all, like sheep, have gone astray, each of us has turned to his own way; and the Lord has laid on him the iniquity of us all.

If you examine the life of Jesus while He was here on earth, it seems that He was always running to the side of someone who was hurting. Down and out people were really attracted to Him, and He gave as much, if not more, of His attention to these people. Rather than spending all of His time and attention on the notable, wealthy and religious of His day, Christ was always in the company of what we might call "undesirables." I thank God, Jesus loved the people nobody else liked.

Some of the groups of people that Jesus befriended were:

- The lame and sick
- Tax Collectors (They were not popular 2,000 years ago either!)
- Lepers
- Prostitutes
- The demon-possessed

I thank God, Jesus loved the people nobody else liked.

There is only one who is good, just and righteous, and that is God. So the only goodness is godliness, and the only righteousness is Christ in [us], which is the hope of glory. God forbid that [we] should boast except in the cross of our Lord Jesus Christ.

Jesus' pattern of constantly running to the side of hurting and neglected people is so important for us, because it works.

I'm not saying we'll beat Him – we know we never will. But we need to run like we can. If we are committed to "racing Jesus," God can use us to share life and hope with others and He will bless us as well.

Rather than spending all of His time and attention on the notable, wealthy and religious of His day, Christ was always in the company of those we might call "undesirables."

Jesus' pattern of constantly running to the side of hurting and neglected people is so important for us because it works. I'm not saying we'll beat Him – we know we never will. But we need to run like we can.

As I look back over my life, the Lord has been so good to me over the years. All my personal dreams have been fulfilled. I wanted to have a family, and have a family that love God, love their children, and love their spouses. I have been so blessed to see that. To God be the glory! I continually thank God because I have been blessed with many wonderful relationships, not only with my wife but with many of God's people. I want my marriage relationship, as well as my other relationships, to be ever growing and to be strengthened in all areas. This will only happen, however, if I pattern my life, and how I run to meet the needs of others, after the example set by Jesus.

Got a "Sticker"? (A Thorn)

Got a "Sticker"? (A Thorn)

My family loves animals. From time to time I like to incorporate lessons that I have learned from pets into my teaching. A lot of those lessons have been learned from Princess, our family's little Dachshund. It is important to know that Princess is no ordinary dog – after all, she is a princess. Princess loves people: she loves being with them, being around them, and if she is in a room full of people, you can hardly get her to stop wiggling because she is so excited at the prospect of new friends. I mean, if you were not understanding, it could get on your nerves, because she is just so excited about seeing you.

Whenever we leave the house, we like to take Princess whenever we can, because she sometimes seems to go into a depression while we are gone. It is the craziest thing in the world, but we even have to explain to her that we are leaving. Just going out to get the mail, when we come back she is hopping and jumping all over the place.

Got a "Sticker"?

It is her way of telling you, "Oh, my! I'm so happy to see you! I'm so glad you came back!"

Now, Princess thinks that she is just like one of the bird dogs that I mentioned earlier. She loves to go sniffing around and checking everything out. She loves being on the go too. When she was a puppy, probably one or two years old, she chased everything that ran. She chased armadillos, but it did not take her long to figure out she could not bite into them, so I would tell her to leave the armadillos alone. Then she chased the deer, but I told her not to chase the deer. "The deer are pretty and I want to keep them around, so do not bother them." Well, then she fell in love with chasing turkeys. She would chase these colorful birds, and finally they would get tired of it and fly away. I forcefully said, "NO! NO! Don't chase turkeys."

Princess loves the adventures of South Texas, but there's one thing there she does not like—stickers (grass burrs). I could be outside with Princess and look up to see this little dog with barely any legs in the first place, limping toward me.

She will have one of her legs pulled up, and her little belly will be dragging on the ground – it really is a sad sight. She will limp over to me, and I will tenderly say, "You got a sticker?" Then I will get the sticker out of her paw.

Sometimes a sticker will break off when I am trying to pull it out. They can be very fine, and even though I think I got all of the sticker out, I can see her licking her little paw. Then she will come limping back over to my chair, and I will take another look. So this time she will get up in my lap and lie on her back and put her little paws up. I turn the light on, look down through my glasses, and try to find the small piece of the sticker still in her paw. Sometimes I even have to get a magnifying glass and use a pair of

Every time Princess comes limping up to me, I always ask, "Got a sticker?" in a concerned tone. I don't think she would ever respond if I yelled at her: "GOT A STICKER? Stupid dog! Stay out of the grass! Quit being a dumb dog! Quit sniffing around all the time! I told you not to go out into the yard!" Too often this is how we respond to people with serious problems in their lives.

tweezers. Eventually I will get the entire sticker out, and after that she is just so happy. She goes running and bouncing all over the place.

One day Princess and I had gone through this process, and I got to thinking about my dream of racing Jesus. Every time Princess comes limping up to me, I always ask kindly, "Got a sticker?" in a concerned tone. I don't think she would ever respond if I yelled at her: "GOT A STICKER? Stupid dog! Stay out of the yard! Quit sniffing around all the time! I told you not to go out into the yard!"

If I were her, I certainly would not respond to the harsh tone. Too often this is how we respond to people with "stickers" (serious problems) in their lives.

Romans 2:4 tells us that God is kind and patient with us so we'll turn from our sin. We should respond like I do with Princess, but we often react by saying "Shame on you! You should be ashamed of yourself! Why were you doing that anyway?" Do we not realize that we all like sheep go astray and get stickers, briars and thorns? If you get a sticker in your life, who are you going to talk to?

What if your sticker was a sexual addiction or same sex attraction? Where would you turn? What about compulsive eating? What about other addictions or hidden sin? So quickly people get on drugs, perhaps prescription, and rather than controlling the use of drugs, the drugs control them – who would you tell if that was your sticker . . . your problem?

I had a wonderful friend who was a heroin addict that I led to Christ, and the Lord freed him from that addiction. He became a great soul winner and evangelist.

Don't you see how wonderfully kind, tolerant, and patient God is with you? Does this mean nothing to you? Can't you see that his kindness is intended to turn you from your sin? (NLT)

Then he got sick, and before he knew it, he was hooked on cough syrup. He would drink the stuff almost like wine, but he never would talk about it because he was embarrassed and ashamed. One day that man had a wreck on the highway because he was under the influence, and he died alone. He had a sticker, and he was afraid to ask for help because he had seen how preachers were treated when they failed. This broke my heart.

Racing Jesus is all about helping those who have stickers, wounds and bruises in life. God help us to have an eye for others who need the compassion of the Father, who need a hand to help them out of the ditch.

We are called to run our race until the day God calls us home. While we run that race, there is only one other person we need to keep our eyes on . . . Jesus Christ. He will keep us running in the right direction, with the right heart and the right words to share with a world in need.

We will never reach the side of the suffering ahead of Jesus, but we should strive to be a close second.

. . . let us throw off everything that hinders and the sin that so easily entangles, and let us run with **perseverance** the race marked out for us. Let us **fix our eyes** on Jesus, the author and perfecter of our faith . . . Hebrews 12:1-2